PUTT
YOURSELF
FIRST

*If just taking time for ourselves is so beneficial to
our health and well-being, why do we do it so little?*

PEA B. LUX

Legal Notice

ISBN: 9798648951594 (Paperback)

Any references to historical events, real people, or real places are used fictitiously. Names, characters, and places are products of the author's imagination.

First printing edition 2020.

Table of Contents

Introduction

"Put on your own oxygen mask before helping others." Nis Arend, founder of the coaching firm The Corporate Confidante, teaches us the golden rule for success: think of yourself first and put your well-being first.

Where do you prioritize your well-being in your life? First, last? No idea?

When we fly, we are always told that in the event of depressurization we must first adjust our own oxygen mask before trying to help others, even children. The explanation is simple: if you cannot breathe, you will not be able to help anyone!

Well, this rule also applies to life in general. When you are called upon from all sides - by your boss, your colleagues, your customers, your friends, your family, and even strangers - it is essential to worry about your balance first.

Keep this rule in mind when you get off the plane and apply it daily.

For years, I myself have had lots of oxygen masks for others, without really worrying about having one for myself. It has taken me a long time to understand that thinking about yourself first is not a selfish act, it is simply vital. I was the person everyone relied on at work, I was the shoulder on which my loved ones poured out, I was the businesswoman, the entrepreneur, the friend, the sister, the aunt, the volunteer, and a thousand other things.

You cannot give more than you have.
So, think about yourself. Set aside time to un-wind and relax. It will feel good and you will be better able to dedicate yourself to others.

Allow yourself to put your well-being first.
In the morning, put yourself in a fighting spirit, both physically and mentally. Start each day with the desire to go after your goals. We know that taking a little time for yourself, even just a few minutes, brings considerable benefits. As soon as you wake up and before you even grab your cell phone, treat yourself to this quality mo-ment with yourself.

You can play sports to keep your mind clear, read a book offering advice on a professional or personal challenge you are facing, or just sit in silence to meditate - the possibilities are endless and at this time it will really help you. Take a step back, relax, and de-stress. You will be more relaxed and serene to start your day with dynamism and motivation.

Make the right choices

If just taking time for ourselves is so beneficial to our health and well-being, why do we do it so little? "I feel guilty" or "I don't know how to do it" are the most common responses. The solution? Review your priority list now and put your well-being first. To do this, we will have to learn to say no and rethink time management. It's not a selfish approach, it's an intelligent one: it will allow you to be more fulfilled and more serene, and it will have positive effects on all aspects of your life.

"I do not have time."

We do not all leave with the same chances in life, but if there is one thing in front of which we are all equal, it is time: whether we are a student or CEO, we all have 24 hours in a day.

If you don't think about yourself first, don't expect others to do it for you.

When they come knocking on the door of my home, my friends are generally in a state of total physical and psychological exhaustion: the concern for their well-being has always come to the forefront, they have forgotten themselves and let themselves be forgotten. Don't get there!

Take charge today, start now: put your well-being first.

Establish your own rituals to feel good and be sure to keep your "time for yourself" every morning, as an important appointment not to be missed.

The best way to develop and nurture a relationship with someone is to spend time with them. What about your relationship with yourself? How much time do you allow yourself each day to feel good?

The next time you fly and the crew reminds you to put on your own oxygen mask first, you will be able to smile secretly because you have already incorporated this rule of survival into your daily life - to feel better, you'll protect yourself and be able to take care of others.

Chapter 1: Putting Yourself First Is Not Selfish

"It is not fair to ask of others what you are not willing to do yourself."

- Eleanor Roosevelt.

Often when people say we are thought of, people around us can accuse us of being selfish. Now, being selfish, what does it mean? Perhaps this adjective is used incorrectly and above all, unjustly. We are going to think about this word, its implications, and how we can spend time for ourselves without feeling guilty. To be selfish is to think of yourself in all circumstances regardless of others.

To understand what it means to be a selfish person, we suggest you rely on the definition given in the dictionary; thus, selfishness would be excessive esteem that a person has for themselves, and which leads them to disproportionately take care of their interest, without worrying about that of the others.

Each of us relies on our own patterns (more or less fixed values and beliefs that we use to interpret the world and get an idea of how it works) and from there start our thoughts. This is why it is not surprising that each person applies this word based on this previous experience and on how they understand the word "selfishness" and its implications. In other words: each person has a different concept of being selfish.

Let us study this story I witnessed many times to fully understand what loving yourself means. There was a woman called Clair who always put people's wellbeing ahead of hers. Her husband, friends, and even strangers. Clair worked 40 hours a week and when she comes home, all that she does is cooking and cleaning. She did not take care of her beauty because she was so busy. One day, unfortunately, her husband asked her for divorce to marry a woman named Lisa who has never had a job and her main priority is putting herself first, taking care of her beauty. Clair's husband paid for Lisa's clothes and necessities from their joint bank account - Clair's and her husband. Lisa doesn't even cook or clean but still, she has the man who fawns over her because she puts herself first.

For some, selfish people are those who have never done anything for them, and for others, in the most extreme case, those who have not granted them a favor due to a lack of time or even though they have been there for them whenever they could. In the first case, the definition given above could be verified... but what about the second case?

How does it feel when a person tells us that we are selfish regardless of all the good things we have done for them? We feel irreparably bad, confused, and angry even if we know that it is unfair. Before we continue, let's make this clear: if we did not do something for someone once when we were asked to do so, that does not mean that we are selfish.

"There is no real happiness in selfishness. "
- George Sand

You Can't Change Other People's Minds

There is a situation that usually recurs often: a person asks us to do something for them and we cannot give them what they need when they ask us to. Subsequently, this person tells us that we are selfish or makes innuendos, and we feel very bad, not only because they have a negative judgment about us, but also because we have found ourselves in a crossroads of interests where ultimately those who we counted on had other agendas for you.

Who acts selfishly, then? Who thinks of themselves without taking into account other people's rights as a person?

There is a clear reality: we do not count on enough resources to try (and not succeed) to change the minds of others. In other words, if a person considers that one act selfishly without trying to understand our circumstances, then one can ask two questions:

- Did we show empathy for their problem?
- Even if we couldn't be there for others when they needed us, is the dynamic of our relationship now sour?

If both answers are yes, never forget this basic freedom: we have the right to reject a request without feeling guilty.

In addition, it is good to take into account that we are making a big mistake if we reduce someone's personality to behavior that they may have had. For example, someone can act mean and not be mean, someone could slip and not be clumsy.

To understand this better, consider the following situation: imagine that you get up at the same time every week. You carry out all the activities that you must carry out and at the end of the day, you have fulfilled all the professional obligations that you had to fulfill. Now imagine that one day you slept an extra 15 minutes and that, for one reason or another, you were not able to do everything you had to do. At the end of the day, you haven't reached all of the goals you set for yourself.

Are you an irresponsible person? Are you a less disciplined person? No, you just had a bad day and you may have acted in an undisciplined and perhaps irresponsible manner. But be aware that because you have acted promptly does not make you a person with these characteristics. Even if you had always done so, in the end, you would not be worthy of these characteristics either because the past does not always predict the present or the future as well.

There is a distinction between acting and being. Being an unfair person is not the same as acting unfairly. Let's analyze the behavior and not the person.

Take advantage of the winds blowing in your favor, but don't let the wind blow you over

Do you feel like you don't have time for yourself? Is there always something happening in people around you that requires your attention and that deviates you from your goals? Do you devote yourself excessively to others? Do you feel like a weather vane at the mercy of the wind? We must always keep a space for ourselves and for this we must learn skills that are fundamental to our well-being: the biggest one is learning to say no without feeling guilty.

There is no doubt that this is something complex and loaded with nuances. This is why we cannot give fixed rules on how we should do it, but rather on the importance of working on it. If you are one of those people who has always been there for others at the expense of your own wellbeing, you should know that:

Change is a Training Process

If we follow a series of habits, changing them will take time, patience, and effort. Normally, our habits are intertwined with each other, and changing one usually involves modifying elements of the whole chain. For example, adopting a more cordial attitude with humanity will require us to know how to converse, whereas before by remaining silent we did not need this ability.

Your friends and family may not understand this: if the people around you are used to having you always say yes to everything, surely, they will be surprised the first time you reject one of their requests. They may even blame you for having changed or for being a "selfish" person. Now is the time where you mustn't forget what you want for yourself. Tell yourself that in the face of change, you will always find resistance, especially if this change involves putting an end to a person's interests.

Always analyze the situation from an objective point of view: if the request of others is not urgent, it does not necessarily require your presence, especially if you have shown empathy towards their problem and if you had offered an alternative arrangement to help them at another time that is compatible with your life and your objectives. In these cases, don't worry, you have no reason to feel guilty.

Finally, thinking of yourself is not being selfish if you now know that it is a balance. If you work on this part of yourself without waiting for the concept and the phrases that touch deeply in our language around selfishness, you will reach a fair degree between devoting time and energy to others and taking care of your passions, your activities, and your dreams.

"Never become a victim. Do not accept the definition of your life for what others tell you. Define yourself." - Harvey Feinstein

Why Should You Think About Yourself Before Thinking Of Others?

In an era of increasingly pronounced individualism, thinking of yourself before thinking of others doesn't sound like good advice, does it? Are we not doing enough already? Well no. Thinking about yourself does not mean a selfish and self-centered withdrawal into your navel. It is a deeper process, which will impact your relationship with yourself and therefore with others. Let's do a check-in.

Alone in the world

You must have heard the phrase "we are always alone in the world". It sounds depressive and slightly apocalyptic, but it is a reality. The only person in the world with whom you are certain to live with until your death is you! So you better deepen the relationship, right? Thinking about yourself, therefore, does not mean being selfish, or worse, withdrawn, it is above all a quest for internal well-being.

Sacrifice at all costs

Our Judeo-Christian culture has instilled in us from a very young age a sense of sacrifice. Sacrifice yourself for others, put aside your desires to please, etc. Instead of creating a society of saints, here we are with a society of suffering martyrs. Not very encouraging. Thinking about yourself is, first of all, listening to yourself and knowing yourself. Too often we pretend to be someone, so much that we end up believing it. By thinking of yourself, I mean reconnecting with yourself to better understand your desires, ambitions, fears, limits, and apply them daily in your choices and actions. No need to sacrifice yourself all the time. If the character like in the movie "Yes Man" have trouble saying yes, most people should learn to say no. A phone call from a friend to have a drink, but you're in the middle of a yoga session and it's cold outside... politely refuse, without having to think of a make-up alternative or making up false excuses. Why shouldn't we have the right to refuse something we don't want?

Energy transmission

Thinking about yourself also means giving off another presence, a new attitude, and a new energy. Some will surely be skeptical, but have you ever felt that your partner or family member was sad or upset without him/her saying anything? This is the energy I'm talking to you about. Our loved ones are often sensitive. However, if my energy is negative because of the choice, of the stress caused by a neglect of oneself, others will feel it. A downward spiral begins: I don't feel good but I don't take care of myself, the others notice it, are will usually question me about it which will trigger me and affect me even more. Do they see that I am troubled? And so on. Taking care of yourself is cultivating this positive energy and having a more positive impact on those around you.

Change the world?

Changing the world is not easy, but if there is one thing that you have an impact on, it is yourself! And it starts with thinking about yourself, knowing yourself, assessing your needs, conflicts, and solving them. Thinking about yourself is not just going to the swimming pool when you want to, cooking good meals, it is also identifying what is wrong and solving it, expressing what you also feel, whether positive or negative. "Care" the idea of a world where you would not hesitate to tell your interlocutor that you feel bad? Or hug a loved one without shame? Maybe maize would be a much healthier world, that's for sure.

Love yourself to love others

And how can you love someone when you don't love yourself? Worst! When you don't know yourself! Thinking about yourself before others are ensuring emotional preparation, balance, and an ability to welcome others into a healthy relationship. We will project on them our fears, our doubts, our beliefs. By knowing our faults, our small faults, we also more easily accept those of others, we judge them less or in a more open and caring manner.

Help yourself first

Finally, you shouldn't lie to yourself. No one will come to do this work for you. If you are tired, exhausted from too much work, too much thunder, too much going out, it is only you who can regulate the rhythm, nobody will stop you and force you to take care of yourself. Your loved ones can motivate you, or run you around tirelessly, you are the one who will ultimately make the decision. You cannot help anyone against your will, which is why it is important to think about yourself, to help yourself before you can help others.

Take action

Thinking about yourself before others should be noted. How? You can apply small recipes from day to day.

Play sports: find the activity that suits you, and too bad if it takes time. Practice it at least 3 times a week. Remember the adage: a mind in a healthy body. Start writing. Without poetry or emphasis. Put what you feel on paper and read it again later when the storm has passed. Or else, take advantage of the blank page to examine yourself and ask a few questions:

- What makes me happy every day?
- Who do I want to see more?
- Who do I want to eliminate from my life?
- What is my biggest dream?
- What is my biggest nightmare?

- What do I think is the meaning of my life?
- What would I want to achieve in 2/5/10 years?
- What steps am I taking towards my goals?

Know how to say real "yes" and real "no". Don't force yourself to go out or do something. We already did it too much in the professional world. Besides, there too, know how to set limits.

It's the little weekly pleasures that keep us grounded. Every Sunday evening, write down on a paper something you want to do during the week, a little pleasure just for you. And do it. Do you understand? Nothing selfish about it. Think of yourself, it will only be beneficial for yourself and others!

Chapter 2: You Are The Only Person Who Lives Your Life

"You don't have to defend or explain your decisions to anyone. It's your life. Live it without apologies"

-Many Hale

Each of us is free to make our own decisions.

We come into this life alone and we die alone. We must be comfortable with being around our selves because, in the end, we are all that we have.

Whether you are single or in a relationship, you have no obligation to explain or justify your choices. If you decide to stop working, have kids (or not have kids), move out, or make any changes in your life, you've probably made that decision after careful consideration.

So, you've taken the time to think about the pros and cons of each of your choices. You also took the time to think about the possible consequences and the expected results. Whatever decision you made; you certainly didn't rush to make this change. So why do you feel the need to justify yourself to others?

You don't have to explain your choices to anyone. Even less to people who have the annoying habit of misinterpreting your actions because they like to judge and criticize. Even less to people who tend to want to keep you trapped in your current situation because it gives them a feeling of security and comfort. Just because someone has a problem with your choice shouldn't stop you from doing it.

Do not sacrifice your happiness because you are afraid of hurting or disappointing others. It would be much worse to live an unhappy life! Either way, people will very rarely be able to understand what you are doing because they don't live for you; they never wore your shoes. They don't know how to touch you emotionally or make you truly happy.

They ignore the fact that you've been waiting for ages to make this change. They do not understand why you are changing certain aspects of your life while leaving others as they are. They don't know your heart: why do you like certain people and not others? Why do you forgive some individuals but not all? They are unable to answer these questions because they are not interested in you but the control of you.

Do you know the adage "Do what I say but don't do what I do?" The people around you will always be ready to give you advice and tell you what to choose, but they very rarely follow their own advice. When it does not directly affect them, these people take things very lightly. They don't care if you're happy or unhappy right now because it doesn't affect their lives in any way.

They do not know your exact situation or your problems and they will not suffer the consequences of your decisions, so why do you care about their opinion? You mustn't stop telling others not to interfere in your life. This is a conscious choice that you have to make: for once, put yourself in the first position. Learn from your mistakes and grow from the decisions you've made.

You are the only one living with the consequences of your choices

Do not become the result of others' choices because if you allow the needs of others to be more important than yours, these people will eventually suffocate you. You are going to be stuck in a life that does not belong to you and that does not reflect your choices or your desires. You will be miserable! And, you should know one thing. Even if you make mistakes, even if you let your emotions get the better of reason, and even if you opt for something that is not in your nature, you do not need the forgiveness of others. You just need to understand what mistakes you have made and try to fix them if possible. If not, you must accept this situation and forgive yourself!

Even if the people around you try to make you believe that they have understood everything in life, this is not the case. They are just as confused as you and they are also continually learning: you cannot trust what they do or what they say. You are the only one who has to live with the consequences of your choices. So, stop defending them.

Stop justifying yourself to people who do not live your life, who do not know your problems, or who do not feel the pain you feel. If you keep listening to them and trying to please them, their opinions and judgments will trap you. You will find yourself living a life that does not suit you. Why would you want this?

Your choices are the only thing that can free you from the grip of others and a miserable life. You don't have to apologize for the decisions you made. If you make a mistake, admit it: keep working on yourself and try to understand why you got there. You owe nothing to others. But you have to be the best you can be.

Each of your choices can turn your life upside down. So, don't let anyone else decide for you for you. Your choice is your choice... No one has the right to interfere in your life. Remember that we come into this life alone and we die alone. Besides, your boyfriend, girlfriend, family, or friends also have no right to criticize or judge your way of life.

You have to be true to yourself because you deserve to be happy. However, if you continue to listen to the opinions of others, to live your life through their eyes, and to be afraid of making your own decisions, you will be unhappy. You'll also lose control of your life and you won't be able to blame anyone but yourself.

Who told you to listen to others? If you live your life according to others, you can only take it out on yourself if you are unhappy or if you have the impression of not being accomplished. Free yourself from this pressure and your fears. You are an amazing and intelligent person: you are perfectly capable of making your own decisions and of bearing the consequences (positive or negative).

Chapter 3: Self-love Is Important To Give Others Love

"A man cannot be comfortable without his own approval."

– **Mark Twain**

Self-love is one of the three components of self-esteem, self-esteem being made up of self-image, self-love, and self-confidence. If there is one area where it is imperative to develop unconditional love, it is good for yourself. Why? Because you can only give what you have. I can give time if I have it, money if I have it, skills if I have them, and I can only give love if I have enough for myself. The great moments of history have been made out of passion and love... Love has always been present in the transformation and evolution of people.

Self-love is not a condition. When we review how we were educated, sometimes we notice that our educators, our teachers, our parental figures, the members of our family who were important to us, out of clumsiness, instilled in us the fact that love is conditioned. How many times have you heard dads or moms say to their kids, "If you love me, finish your plate."? What is the relationship between the fact that I refuse to finish my plate because I am no longer hungry with the fact of continuing to be loved by you? Imagine that a simple exchange like this can create a drama!

A child, when he hears this sentence, understands that to be loved, he must do something! To be loved, he must conform to what the other wants and not to his own need. And very early in our education, we set up systems that relate self-love to something conditioned.

Take the example of a husband who says to his wife, "If you love me, get rid of your extra 10 pounds." This expression makes this person believe that she is unworthy and does not deserve to be loved. As a result, the day she needs love, she will throw herself on food because she has created a cause and effect association with it. Because we all need to love and be loved. The sentence that should be said would be, in this case: "Whatever happens, I love you! "

To love yourself unconditionally is also to love yourself with all your faults. Your inner child wants you to love him completely and unconditionally. I was preparing a journal on nonverbal language and very late at night, on an obsolete channel, there was a report on death row, and a serial killer who had killed 4 people in incredibly violent circumstances. The killer was tied to his chair for the execution and the families of the dead victims walked past him and cursed him. He was receiving all forms of violence... but what was surprising was that there was no sign of compassion on his face. One could even see, on analysis of nonverbal language, micromovements which generated discontent. As one behind the other marched to insult him. The second last person was a grandmother, who came with a trembling hand, grabbed her hand and said to the prisoner: "You took my only little girl away from me, it was a jewel, an exceptional beauty. I forgive you; God forgives you! At that moment, when she wanted to withdraw her hand, the criminal grabbed her hand, fell in tears, apologized to this woman, and everyone... I found this scene extraordinary!

How a human being can express a little love towards a "monster" so that he responds, becomes aware of what he had done, and asks to be executed because he deserved it. It's the power of love!

You should love yourself by eliminating the "I love myself if..." "Or" I will love myself when... .. "and replace them with an" I love myself because I am someone who deserves it ". At no time condition the love you have for yourself.

You are a unique being and you must love yourself!

When you set up appointments with yourself for a sports session, meditation, training, or lunch with a friend, and for some reason X, unfortunately, you cannot assure it: do not cancel it! Postpone but do not cancel this appointment. Studies have shown that in 90% of the cases studied, individuals do not postpone when it comes to themselves... They cancel! "Others" should not be more important than "yourself" … Love yourself for what you are. Tell yourself that you are only one representation of what you are in the world. One piece... A masterpiece! When you have finished reading my book, I ask you to say to yourself regularly: "I love you! " It is not a question here of egocentricity exacerbated even less of narcissism but unconditional love of oneself. It makes you want to realize yourself, motivates, gives you desires for greatness, and desires to contribute to a better world.

"Our thoughts about who we are and what we can be determined precisely what we can be." Anthony Robbins says.

Loving yourself is not necessarily self-evident. Our image is, however, fundamental to structure our behavior. And, through that, our relationship with others.

The importance of loving yourself

At first glance, however, the idea of loving yourself seems futile, ridiculous as if there was nothing more important in existence! - or very pretentious. Traditionally and culturally, the emphasis is on the ability to love others. But modern psychology tells us a very different story. She posits that loving yourself a minimum is essential to experience pleasure and find charm in life. It is enough to imagine the days of someone who would get up every morning finding himself stupid and ugly, convinced of his inferiority and his unworthiness to be loved. It is easy to deduce that his emotional and professional life would be an ordeal.

For the psychologist William James (1842-1910), self-love is the product of a sufficiently small gap between our ambitions and our actual successes. However, the most recent research rejects this realism, showing that it is better not to have a too lucid vision of oneself and one's true abilities.

American psychiatrists Robert Ornstein and David Sobel, who have given the fruits of their research on self-image in "The Virtues of Pleasure" (Laffont, 1992) affirm that "happiness is the privilege of those who know how to cultivate positive illusions, and can consider themselves smarter and more competent than they are ". Do you firmly think that your boss appreciates you especially when, for him, you are only an average employee? So much the better! Someone tells you their opinion about you, finding you stingy but charming, domineering, brilliant, and a little aggressive. If you are a balanced person, you will remember "charming", "brilliant" and, possibly, "aggressive".

"Overestimating yourself and immediately forgetting disturbing qualifiers is beneficial," said Robert Ornstein and David Sobel. Our vision of ourselves is just a construction of our minds. It is therefore up to us to make it as pleasant as possible, while of course avoiding sinking into megalomania. Perfectly realistic individuals are always slightly depressed. "

Recognize a certain value

Psychology dictionaries define self-love by a set of attitudes: recognizing a certain value, taking care of oneself, protecting one's private territory, one's physical and mental health, knowing one's real interests. It's about being a "good mother" for yourself.

But if self-love manifests itself in the actions we take, it is, first of all, a matter of inner experience, of personal feeling. I can estimate myself intellectually, have confidence in myself, while hardly supporting my physical appearance. A relatively positive vision of oneself in no way excludes that one blames oneself for one or more particular character traits or certain intellectual flaws - lack of courage, ambition, or tenacity for example.

An American study carried out in 1993 based on a questionnaire sent to several hundred people between 20 and 30 years old and directed by the researcher James Overholser, confirmed that men and women have criteria of appreciation of them- some different - what we suspected a little. The former love themselves through their successes, professionally or through physical activity, while the latter have a visceral need for those around them to recognize their personal qualities.

It is exceptional to fully accept yourself; everyday life proves it. This dissatisfaction, inherent in human nature, makes it possible to believe that existential fullness is not a myth. And that it would have been enough for us to enjoy it.

Love and adapt to others

Loving yourself implies an ability to not only care about yourself and not to take responsibility in front of others based on considerations of style: "You take me completely as I am or goodbye. "It's even the reverse. Self-love supposes a good dose of awareness, of knowledge of one's mental functioning. It goes hand in hand with the ability to adapt to the needs of others, without alienating them, and with the ability to transform when necessary.

The judgments we make about ourselves depend on how we perceive life. Hence the naivety of the speeches which enjoin us not to worry about the opinion of others. To ignore them completely is impossible, even if we have some leeway.

The gap between me and me

With ourselves, the relationship is hardly more peaceful. At 8 a.m., the mirror sends me a reflection that suits me, but nothing says that it will be the case at the end of the day. A stranger jostles me in the subway, a problem at work prompts me, for a flash, to question my skills, and immediately my relationship to my image deteriorates, and dark memories, negative judgments come to my mind.

Why this gap between me and me? Paradoxically, there is nothing innate about this self that we consider our most intimate and private good. Fetus then infant, we are deprived of it. The ego is built in the relationship with our first "others": our mother, our father, or those who take their place.

According to psychoanalyst Jacques Lacan, it was around the age of 18 months - at the time of the "mirror stage" - that it began to develop. It is the adult who raises this awareness in the child by showing him his image in the mirror and especially by commenting: "You see, there, in the mirror, it is you. And he is laughing and gloating with pleasure while recognizing himself. The child who has missed this test of self-recognition can have terrible anxiety attacks when the ice sends him back his image: he is a terrifying and unlovable creature whom he then sees. To love yourself, you still have to know that you exist as a distinct individual.

Why meditate?

Many of us have realized that the experiences we have had remain superficial. They did not lead to happiness with the feeling that there was a dimension missing. There is an aspiration towards a better elsewhere.

Often, an inner impulse, like an intuition, has led us step by step to become aware of the need to deepen our life experience. We want to improve the quality and develop our ability to create and cultivate. What are we looking for first?

Tranquility, well-being, and calm.

It sounds simple a priority and it is, but accessing this immediacy is not easy, especially as the busy Westerners that we are. We are so used to complicating our existence, totally identified with the problems, the agitation, and the mind mill. It keeps getting something to grind on, and it can be hard to imagine living without it. Meditation represents at the beginning of making efforts. Then, we enjoy it as we go forward and we feel its many benefits.

WHAT ARE THE 5 FOOL-PROOF PHASES OF MEDITATION?

There are several levels of depth of well-being and calm, a bit like on a frequency scale on which you can go up and down. Below is the best method of mediation that I created to help guide you.

1) The body or physical posture

The first level is that of the physical body. It is our basic vehicle from which we can send and receive, and open up to all kinds of experiences. In this case, we are opening up to the energy and space of peace and harmony of the great universal spirit of life. And breathing is the bridge, the one that connects us to the body and life. Like any vehicle, you have to take care of it and give it that kind of permeability and transparency. We must take care of our bodies with a healthy diet and proper exercise. Thus, we preserve health and vitality. We prepare and feel the openness that gives access to this essential.

One thing to remember is that the more you learn to relax your body, the deeper you can go into the meditation experience.

Posture in itself matters little in the end. It must be essentially comfortable to help you achieve an adequate level of well-being and relaxation. So of course, we have in mind this picture of the perfect lotus posture of the Buddha. It's a strong symbol of balance and alignment; however, you need to be pragmatic. Your practice should be adapted to your lifestyle.

How can we get peace of mind if we are not comfortable with our bodies? We could well meditate standing or in an armchair, legs and arms well relaxed... or lying on a sofa or a bed... which is important to know how to meditate. With a little practice, everything becomes meditation.

2) The lake of unthought

Do you know that to stop thinking is the highest way of thinking? Not so easy! And yet, what could be more refreshing, when you think about it than not thinking anymore!

We must accept that our intellect has its limits. You should also know that the thinking function of our brain is only useful for certain things. It is useful in the orbit of what it is made for and what it can do. It's about making yourself fully available and opening up to something new. We open up to this stranger, which can only mirror itself on the lake of tranquility.

How to do it?

• The best is to close your eyes, to focus your attention on breathing. You are comfortably installed.

• In this phase, it is important to understand what it means to step back and let go. This allows us to settle in a kind of transparency, neutrality. We look at the clouds - thoughts that cross our sky - without ever hanging on them, without attaching to them. Neither should we judge them or argue with them. We don't feed them. It's a great basic exercise.

• As soon as you realize that you have allowed yourself to be off-center by one of them, return to the center quietly. Come back to your breathing... persevere!

If you are not trained at all, start with 1 to 5 minutes in the morning and the evening...

At first, it takes effort, and the mind will find a thousand and one excuses to turn you away from it. Then, when we start to enjoy it because we feel good doing it, our meditation times will naturally lengthen. As time goes by, the flow of thoughts and mental agitation will weaken until it gradually disappears, at least on the surface. You will not have allowed yourself to be dominated by the merry-go-round and the gear of the mind.

Your mind will soon capitulate if you don't give it a hold. It no longer finds material to grind, while from your center, you are no longer identified with this surface noise. You have applied the correct distance. Things no longer control you. You have broadened the scope of your usual perception. Apply micro-meditation at a convenient time during the day. Whether it's in a queue or a waiting room, for example, or in a busy shopping area... It will become automatic and natural.

3) Dharana: focus on one thing

In this phase, it is important to have already reached a certain level of inner calm and silence. It is about going deeper, and in a feeling of both self-esteem and humility. We are going to touch our own source. It's a bit like letting things go up and revealing their content, their truth.

It is a kind of deep self-reflection, a means of self-observation that allows us to patiently discover. We discover with the help of our Being, the light of the star which, from the inside always smiles and guides us. This light guides us to take a closer look at what is playing out in us. It is about inspecting false beliefs and prejudices that we have about ourselves. Likewise, we can identify the psychological aspects that block us in our desire to change our lives. It's like extracting the quintessence and understanding the hidden springs of our psychology and behavior patterns. It is a question of restoring order in our psyche and in our life without which no change can be carried out.

And, it is not so much the external circumstances in themselves that interest us, but what they have to reveal to us. These are the root causes of our actions and our words. These are our fears, our beliefs, and everything related to the conditioning of consciousness. This goes as far as observing our mental prison in the different levels of the subconscious.

4) Deep meditation

After taking the necessary step back and having reached a certain level of calm in practice, we can move forward. We can rise. The free and natural movement of consciousness is to "go straight up" on this journey. And this, until a certain form of stabilization in a luminous sphere which one could qualify as nirvanic. We settle deeper and deeper in the heart of our temple where everything is serene depth. Our soul cannot resist it and we only have one desire... to stay there, to prolong it.

We let ourselves be thought of by "God" himself in a way. Things are happening in us to a depth that our poor intellect could never have access to. We also need to let things happen in peace. Things are falling into place. It's like something else has taken over, something in you that knows what you need. You can then let yourself be guided with confidence, obtain information, and live this communion with your intimate... where you allow yourself to bloom in a form of bliss irresistible bliss. This is how we can arrive at the fifth phase which we could believe to be a summit in meditation.

5) Ecstasy, Samadhi or illuminating emptiness

It's not going to be easy to express what this notion of vacuum illuminator is. It is a full void where you are all in one, dissolved as if melted into the Unity of free life in its movement. You are then the living water, the bird, the wind, the rain, the air, the earth, and the fire living at the heart of everything... It is a sublime and irresistible experience it is true, where you bathe in ineffable love and joy. Go there without getting lost.

However, in dazzling this impersonal unitary trance, we can lose ground - having experienced it myself - and come back no more advanced than before. We can come back even slightly disabled. You can get a kind of disease that Zen Buddhists call "Satori disease" where you sort of fall asleep in this state.

"Ecstasy could be a higher form of unconsciousness," said Sri Aurobindo. And, what we call absolute, transcendent would then only be the limit of our current consciousness. The term "ecstasy" always evokes this exterior, like a light and temporary escape from the soul at a privileged moment. However, nothing guarantees in this surge, the real and stable acquisition of internal values. This is why it can never be seen as an end or a peak in itself.

Increasing awareness

It's about being more and more aware of balance and alignment between mind, energy, and matter. What is interesting is to become this channel and to solidly and consciously realize this bridge between heaven and earth.

If we rave too long, we risk losing sight of "someone in us." Someone who can make this bridge between the powers from above and what can be done from below.

The blind leap into the absolute, we are tempted to do it by closing our eyes. We want to rush into these ineffable regions where we certainly enjoy a state of bliss. It's, not against, just as blind because once we come back, we don't remember anything, because we're unconscious.

What is interesting is to live the joy of contact with the highest dimensions without getting lost or falling asleep. This is where we enter the field of integrative "en-stasis" where, as a conscious investigator of our regions, we return with clarity of experience. We see everything we have experienced, done, heard. We remember our conversations with the Angel or with God, which then becomes a concrete reality of life. And this, in addition, in the waking state, eyes wide open.

In conclusion, it is important to let yourself go through each step at your own pace. It is necessary to master the inner calm before being allowed to explore further. I invite you to start (or continue) meditation to see the benefits in turn.

Chapter 4: Guilt And Pity Is Manipulation

"Nobody knows what God's plan is for your life, but a whole lot of people will guess for you if you let them."

— **Shannon L. Alder**

If it is still painful, the guilt is not necessarily negative. It is a structuring emotion, which promotes empathy, and a useful benchmark between good and evil. "Guilt is an unpleasant emotional experience, characterized by a feeling of tension, anxiety, and restlessness, writes Laurent Bègue, social psychologist. But, well before constituting an inappropriate manifestation, it is a sign of good psychological health. "It signals to us that we have acted badly, transgressed our values, our moral principles.

For example, I'm always mad at myself when I'm getting impatient at a supermarket cashier. I had the choice to do otherwise, to be patient; and I don't like to lose my self-control or hurt others. So, I regret the words or thoughts I had for someone just trying to do their job. "The memory of the torments which accompany guilt incites us to be loyal, to treat others well, humans or animals," confirms Laurent Bègue in his essay. It makes us more empathetic, more sensitive to their suffering, quicker to apologize. It would, therefore, be a useful safeguard to stay on the right path, a structuring emotion, guarantor of our consciousness of good and evil. However, we see it in everyday life, our feeling of guilt rarely makes us move forward on these reasonable and empathetic paths. On the contrary, it is often the cause of unnecessary anxiety. Especially since our feelings alone do not allow us to distinguish useful guilt from its destructive counterpart.

A universal emotion

It is not a question of valuing the total absence of guilt, characteristic of the psychopath, for whom other people are only an object. According to the psychoanalyst Jacques Lacan, like anger or joy, it belongs to the most universal and archaic effects, those which appear in an almost innate way. According to the psychoanalyst Melanie Klein, one of the main specialists in early childhood, it manifests itself from the first months of life and results from the ambivalence of the feelings experienced for the mother.

Because we tend to get lost between reality and imagination, we are all condemned for guilt, including for acts that we will never commit (killing our father, mother, neighbors, or office colleagues who bother us), including lending others feelings they may not have in return.

A too idealized vision of ourselves also pushes us to feel our failures as moral faults:

> *"I am angry with myself because I am not as good as I should be. Worse still, we can be tortured by unconscious guilt that we do not perceive, but which leads us towards the behavior of failure or which makes us sick. In the case, there was no question of relying on the superego, the internalized moral conscience, to serve as a benchmark. Indeed, generally too severe, it always asks us more - "Give up your pleasures",* ***"Think of others before thinking of you"****, "You should have succeeded much better", "You take pleasure in your mediocrity", etc.*
> ***Why should I think of others before thinking of myself?***

According to Jacques Lacan, some of us go so far as to commit petty crimes (running a red light, stealing from the supermarket...) to finally have a good reason to feel at fault. And the proof being contrary exists. Guilt is so quick to arise in each of us that guilt is one of our best tools for influencing the other and making them act the way we want:

"Don't you have time to come see me? It does not matter. You'll come when I'm dead," sighs this grandmother at her granddaughter.

A deceptive feeling

However, feeling guilty never proves that it is justified. Between the guilt according to the law and the mental capability of the person behind the guilt. As proof, the famous guilt of a plane crash survivor: "I am alive while all the other passengers of the plane perished", "I am in full health while my child is sick".

The mother who entrusts her baby to a nanny to go to the movies sometimes feels worse than the motorist who accidentally hit a pedestrian or the serial killer who slit the throats of fifty women.

A woman who puts herself first will be seen as guilty.

Why this palette of feelings before the action? Because nothing is more complicated than de-limiting the border between good and bad be-havior. Thus, according to the philosopher Em-manuel Kant, lying is always evil. Now, was not lying to save the innocent, as the righteous did during the Second World War, on the contrary, not a respectable act? And we like to believe that some of those who hastened to collaborate have been tortured with guilt. Besides, behaving following the law does not even protect us from the inner, physical discomfort of this lump in the throat that this feeling creates.

An episode from the television series The Closer: L.A. Priority Investigations provides a perfect example. Chef Brenda Leigh Johnson is plagued by guilt as she provokes a confession from a young pregnant woman who has murdered an entire family in the belief that she is protecting the father of her child. She has arrested a murderer, but must now take responsibility for bringing a baby to prison, who will then be taken from her mother and placed in social care. This is, of course, a fiction, but for all of us, we have to deal with such dilemmas daily. Without having other benchmarks than our consciousness, our idea of good and evil is always varied.

We feel guilty about going to a club hotel in Punta Cana instead of spending all the holidays in the countryside with our sick mother. But we do it anyway, sometimes going so far as to self-punish by forbidding us to take advantage of this moment of relaxation. Let's also think of the classic story of the man who made his mistress wait for years by swearing that he was going to leave his wife. But not now, because he feels bad at the mere mention of leaving the marital home: the wife needs him too much... His guilt simplifies his existence and spares him a challenge in his way to live.

Another example is Suzan's story. Susan's mother calls her and asks her if she can babysit her siblings this weekend. Susan has plans or just didn't feel like doing it. Well her mother starts bringing up guilt tactics to use such as "I would do it for you", "When you were a baby, I took care of you"," I cannot imagine that you will be a mother one day" etc. It is not Susan's responsibility but it is selfish from her mother's part to try and manipulate her into not putting herself first.

Lacan asserts that the only thing we can be guilty of is not to assume our desires, to be "morally cowardly." He does not speak of whims or sexual impulses to be sated on the spot, even less of criminal or perverse tendencies, but of the vital force which drives our existence. It is, for example, the desire to paint or write that pushes artists to create despite hunger or poverty. More on a daily basis, it's the desire to be independent, to exercise a profession that we like, to have our time, to love who we want - beyond the criticism of those around us. That is to say that the exit from guilt goes through self-knowledge, and the recognition of our true desires and possible errors. By our ability to assert "I want", "I assume". By accepting our responsibility for our aspirations and our actions. The more we try to run away from the dark or socially incorrect aspects of our ego, the more we sink into guilt.

Guilt, shame, embarrassment

The guilt results from the transgression, real or imagined, of a moral rule (to make suffer, to lie, to deceive, to steal, to kill...). It concerns our relationship with the law. When we feel guilty, we try to fix it. Shame is linked to the fear of social rejection, of exclusion. It results from the feeling of being unworthy, inferior to others (because one is in misery, illiterate, uncultivated...). We feel it if we wear mundane clothes on a swanky evening, or when, poor, we are surrounded by wealthy people, for example. It makes us want to run away, to hide. Embarrassment arises when we contravene conventions, rules of good manners (not burping, farting, walking around with the fly open or scratching your buttocks in public, etc.). embarrassed to put ourselves first before others, we apologize.

GUILT, THE BIGGEST CAUSE OF DISEASE

So far, I have had the opportunity to teach and have had to face the fact that everyone, without exception, regardless of culture, religion, age, job, sex lives with a lot of guilt. Lack of love has become a scourge all over the world.

Guilt plays a big part in the unpleasant situations we live in. In general, what is most harmful is the lack of awareness of our guilt. Most people are aware of between 5% and 10% of what is going on inside them, and the same unpleasant incidents are repeated over and over. This is why my primary motivation is to provide tools to help them develop their awareness.

To feel guilty is to believe that you are at fault. But putting yourself first is not a fault at all. Either we feel guilty or we try to make others feel guilty when they allow themselves to be what we think is wrong. So, it's very important to be alert to what's going on inside you. Be aware that as soon as you feel any discomfort, there is a 90% chance that you will feel guilty toward yourself but don't surrender and put others before you.

Ways to become more aware when you feel guilty.
In addition to causing us internal discomfort, guilt is also the cause of many ailments and illnesses. A physical problem that is causing slight pain is a sign of guilt. It's an unconscious means that you use to punish yourself, believing you are a bad person.

Look where it hurts and link it to the usefulness of that part of your body to get a clue about the cause of the guilt. For example, if you have sore legs, which are necessary to move forward, then you have to look at what you are accusing yourself of or what you are after in your way of moving forward. You just have to give yourself the right not to be able to do and be what you want at the moment. Your body's messages always tell you to accept what you don't like about yourself and not to change. Any change in your life can only happen when you accept your limits, that is, what you do not like to be. It's the only way to be what you want to be not what others want.

• When you feel guilty about someone, you may realize that what you think they are is a reflection of your judgment. So, you learn that you blame yourself to the same degree when you dare to be what you judge.

Guilt...or I put myself first
It shows that you are asking too much for the moment. You forgot that to truly love yourself is to give yourself the right to live all kinds of experiences as a human being to learn about yourself.

I may draw your attention to the fact that you are not implementing the concept of responsibility. To be responsible is to know that we constantly create our lives according to our decisions, our actions, and our reactions. It is also knowing that it is we who must bear the consequences. Being responsible also means remembering that others create their own lives and that it is up to them to take responsibility for their own consequences.

As soon as guilt manifests in your life, you can become aware that it is no longer you who rule your life, but your ego to which you give too much power. Only the ego believes in good and evil. When we are in our hearts, instead of judging ourselves, we observe ourselves and have compassion for the human limits that we all have.

According to your ego, if you blame yourself a lot, you are more likely to improve, when in reality it is the opposite. For example, if you are an angry person, have you noticed that the more you accuse yourself and promise to stop being so, the more you start again. It's the same thing when we feel guilty about others: our ego believes it will help them not to do it again when we all know it is wrong.

The antidote to guilt: enforcing the law of responsibility. By accepting the consequences of your actions, you learn what is smart for you and what is not. So, instead of viewing an action as bad or a mistake, you become thankful that you can use it to help you steer more towards an intelligent attitude.

Take the example of being angry. To be responsible and to love yourself is to ask yourself what are the harmful consequences for you of being angry. Take the time to become aware of it. Then decide what you want in this situation. It fits your need. It may be that you speak calmly. Whatever your answer, say thank you to this part of you for helping you discover a need. The most important thing is to realize whether the decisions are smart and beneficial for you or not. By keeping in mind what you want, you can slowly start doing different things while giving yourself the right to take the time it takes to fill your need. The only way to be what we want is to give ourselves the right to be what we don't want, without charge or guilt.

Victimization

Victimization is a pattern of behavior that creates an obstacle to authentic relationships. But how can you recognize it? The goal is not to put a label, but rather to understand how sub-persons act without our knowledge, including that of the Victim.

What is a subpersonality?

Subpersonality is a model of survival that came into being when we needed it to survive our unfulfilled needs. It is present and manifests in the form of constellations of behaviors, feelings, or thoughts that have crystallized to help us survive our unmet needs.

If you are one of those people who often lose control of their lives, who cannot defend themselves, if you allow outside forces or other people to influence your life or tend to feel self-pity, you may have a profile of the victim.

The Victim is that person who easily lets themselves be dominated by others or by external events, thus losing the power of their life, which is often complex, arduous, and strewn with painful, even dramatic events. Not feeling clever enough, strong enough to defend herself, she relies heavily on those around her and is easily found under the influence of others until she is subjected to it, which will prevent her from adequately meeting her own needs. "Why me" - "It is because of..." - "It is not my fault" -

"Yes, but..." are part of her verbal language while her body language manifests this state of victimization by sighs, eyes raised to the sky, hunched back and swinging arms, and/or an oscillating contemplation of the ground.

The victim is found in people who, within their family structure, have developed great dissatisfaction, an emotional deficiency, and repressed frustration. Victim of abuse, whether it be physical, psychological, emotional, sexual, or spiritual abuse, her self-esteem depends on her ability to suffer more than anyone. She, therefore, maintains the belief that life is difficult and that suffering is the only way to feel normal. Besides, it is easily found in situations that help to strengthen this belief.

Unconsciously, the Victim lives in fear of failing, losing control, displeasing, being rejected, or abandoned. She has a negative perception of herself, believing herself weak and incapable. She also experiences a feeling of helplessness in the face of all the negative rules, harmful messages, prohibitions and limitations of the family nucleus, which will cause her to feel inferior and to live in shame and guilt. She also experiences a great feeling of injustice and apathy, causing her to react as if everyone wanted to abuse her. Paradoxically, she attracts people who abuse her or seek to dominate her, in such a way that her romantic partner can behave like a persecutor. Indeed, tired and irritated by the behavior of the Victim, the Persecutor (rebellious victim) may develop aggressiveness, frustration, or even physical or verbal violence or any other harmful attitude towards her. Besides, the victim often becomes excessively attached to her persecutor.

Her attitude of "martyrdom" also leads the Victim to reject responsibility for her life and to hand it over to her spouse, her family, and those around her. And here we come back to putting others before us. The Victim has a great capacity for complaining and attracting pity but also has a strong tendency to criticize, accuse, and blame the other, which is another aspect of power.

Do you recognize yourself as a Victim?

If you:
☐ let outside forces control your life
☐ easily feel sorry for yourself
☐ can't count on yourself
☐ feel that you lack efficiency
☐ lack self-confidence
☐ are often losing control of your life
☐ are influenced by the will of others

☐ let yourself go and let yourself be annihilated
☐ always seek reassurance, approval
 easily complain
☐ dramatize situations

You probably have the behavior of the victim. Fortunately, the good news is that you can enter into a positive transformation process to bring balance back into your life and a therapeutic approach (psychotherapy, therapeutic hypnosis) can help you achieve this goal.
How to identify that the victim's scheme is over?

You then realize that you:

☐ are now responsible for your life
☐ welcome your emotions and feelings as allies and no longer as adversaries.
☐ recognize your inner power
☐ transform your beliefs and perceptions so that they adjust to your reality
☐ develop greater confidence in others
☐ wait until you are respected in words, gestures, actions
☐ are open to yourself and others
☐ stop projecting your discomfort onto others
☐ develop your true self
☐ dare to take risks

Positive and effective professional help will allow you to pacify yourself with life to better live in the present while helping you to finally regain the power of your life. Dare to take the risk of transforming things, you can only benefit!

We all use manipulation... 97% of us someday sooner or later. For the remaining 3%, however, manipulation has become a strategy, a deliberate act. The manipulation provides a feeling of power, which reassures the manipulators. But why is it so difficult to outsmart the traps of the manipulators? This is the question we will answer in this book. To manipulate a person is to make that person do something that he does not intend to do, without realizing that he is being made to do this thing like the example of Suzan who was manipulated by her mother.

Manipulation is, therefore, an action that victims undergo. The manipulation causes unpleasant emotions in these victims, such as sadness, guilt, fear, or even discouragement. It is often when you wonder about these emotions that you become aware of the manipulation. But often one experiences these unpleasant feelings without really understanding what is going on or what is causing it. When the manipulation is subtle, one does not even have the impression of being, or of having been manipulated. Manipulation can therefore only exist if there are two: the manipulator and the manipulated. By choosing not to be manipulated anymore, and by choosing to assert ourselves, we can, there-fore, outwit the manipulators. We can stop be-ing their victims. You just have to learn how.

I've been manipulated and so have countless other people. For example, a 50-year-old man who has never been married and has no kids who pretends that he is a Medical Doctor online to get into the pants of 20-year-old women only for them to realize that he is not a certified MD but his title in the medical field is much less. He manipulates these young women into thinking he is someone who he is not. These women are interested in what he can provide them in life but he is interested in free sex. The prostitutes he visits charge him whereas naive women can be tricked out of it. By telling them he is a doctor and burdening them with his problems, they display empathy for him. Sympathy for this man whose *"never met the right person"*. In reality, he probably meets the "*right person*" every month. At some point after being used, the women analyze the situation and conclude that he is the problem in his life and he will continue to remain stagnant and nothing good shall come unto him. Then they continue with their lives as he continues to gather spells of D.U.M.E upon him which manifests. If he would have been upfront about it he would not have been able to manipulate them and his life would possibly be better.

How does a manipulator do it?

The principle of manipulation is simple: the manipulator touches a sensitive cord of his victim, which causes internal pain in this victim. The manipulator can choose between two types of sensitive strings. There is a chord that causes an unpleasant feeling: guilt, pity, fear, sadness, etc. And there is the chord that suggests unpleasant consequences.

Let's see this through examples of manipulation: The manipulator cries to soften you when you are angry. You feel sorry for the tears of the other person. It's an unpleasant emotion. The manipulator howls until he gets what he wants. I can't stand the screams anymore. If it's my child screaming in a supermarket, I'm embarrassed or ashamed of other people. These are unpleasant sensations.

The manipulator makes the victim generate a feeling of guilt within themselves: "Because of you, I..."
- I feel responsible or guilty for what happens to the other person (unpleasant feeling)

- The manipulator sulks until he gets what he wants
- I suffer from his silence (unpleasant feeling)
- The manipulator flatters you before making a request
- I am delighted by the compliment and do not want to disappoint the flatterer (unpleasant consequence)

Why do we let ourselves be manipulated?

The victim of a manipulator has two choices:

☐ she can refuse manipulation, and then suffer the painful consequences that this implies;

☐ or she can agree to let herself be manipulated, which is easier, and less unpleasant (a priori...)

When the victim is not aware of the manipulation, they choose to let themselves be manipulated. Because they hope to stop this inner suffering that the manipulator has created in them. Because they think they are escaping unfortunate consequences.

If I take the examples above:

The manipulator cries to soften you when you are angry "I'm ashamed to make him cry. I was too hard. I can't stand to see him cry. I'd rather be quiet than see him in this state".

The manipulator howls until he gets what he wants.

"I can no longer bear the screams of this child. So, I give in so I don't hear them screaming anymore". It's less difficult (in the short term.)

The manipulator makes the victim generate a feeling of guilt in you: "Because of you, I..."
I'm ashamed of what I told him. It hurt him a lot, I feel guilty. I prefer to apologize and withdraw my remarks, then to feel this guilt. The manipulator sulks until he gets what he wants from me, it would be more unpleasant to disappoint him, than to do what he asks me. Of course, to accept manipulation is to think in the short term. Because the manipulator will know that manipulation works on us. Then he will start again. Again. And again. In his company, we will feel strange, painful feelings. We will feel guilty, we will be sad, we will be afraid, we will be discouraged, etc. The consequences of manipulation are far more harmful in the long run.

Chapter 5: You Deserve The Best

"You deserve the best, the very best, because you are one of the few people in this lousy world who are honest to themselves, and that is the only thing that really counts."

— Frida Kahlo

The blur. Here is a weapon that the manipulators master; here is a weapon that the manipulators use against us. How do they use it? And how can we protect ourselves from them? I explain all this and give you 5 practical tips.

Why are the manipulators in the dark?
The vagueness presents 5 major interests for the manipulators:

By expressing themselves in vague terms, the manipulators let us interpret their words. So, they can change their mind more easily. By remaining vague, the manipulators do not engage. This allows them to take responsibility.
By being blurred, the manipulators allow themselves some leeway. They can, therefore, hide their game, and prevent it from being discovered.

By being deliberately incomprehensible
through a "cultivated" discourse, the manipulators give themselves importance and power.

The vagueness causes a kind of mystery around the manipulator. This mystery can sometimes seduce us.

How do the manipulators stay in the dark?

To stay in the dark, manipulators use several techniques. For example, Manipulators don't finish their sentences. They let us interpret their words. That way they can always say, "I never said that. " Manipulators use ambiguous formulations or words, which can have several meanings.

They use a very specific vocabulary that we will not understand. They do it on purpose: their goal is precisely to be incomprehensible. We dare not show our embarrassment for fear of exposing our (so-called) ignorance. In this way, the manipulators give themselves authority.

Communicating with a manipulator is, therefore, an ordeal. We have to be on our guard. In traditional communication, the goal is to exchange clear and precise ideas. Everyone's goal is to understand and be understood.

The manipulator does not share this point of view at all. As we have just seen, the manipulator will try to stay in the dark. You must, therefore, be vigilant. Here are 5 tips that I would like to share with you. I'm sure they will help you with the manipulators around you:

Don't let anything go

Learn to recognize each manipulation attempt. And react systematically. Don't let anything go by. Replicate tick to tick with each remark. By reacting like this, you show that you are not fooled. The manipulator will quickly understand who he is dealing with and will use his manipulation on someone else.

Blur out

Whenever a manipulator tries to stay in the dark, make it clear: The manipulators make evasive or ambiguous sentences: rephrase his ambiguous sentence and ask him to validate: "Is that what you are telling me? " Manipulators imply: ask him to be specific: "What do you mean exactly? " The manipulators do not commit: make him take a position as you go: "What are you going to do concretely? " The manipulators hijack the conversations and end up getting lost: come back to the real topic of the conversation: "My original question was xxx, but I think you haven't answered it yet. I would like you to answer it now. "

Say no

You must learn to say no, without justifying yourself. To help you do this, you can use the scratched disc technique. This technique consists of repeating the same sentence, calmly and patiently, each time the manipulator insists. This sentence is for example: "I understand, but it is not. ", quite simply.

Control your emotions

I already talked about it in this book asserting yourself against manipulators, the manipulators try to make you feel unpleasant emotions: guilt, shame, fear, etc. Do not be fooled, and try to see clearly in the game of the manipulator.

Understand that you feel this unpleasant feeling through manipulation.

Understand how the manipulator succeeded in making you feel these emotions. Wait some time to make your decision without taking these emotions into account.

Love yourself and let yourself be loved

It is essential to do things that we love, to take advantage of the opportunities that come our way without thinking about it too much, without too high expectations, simply with the will to live and to express life.

For this, it is fundamental to love yourself and to let yourself be loved.

Loving yourself is complicated, but it is a fundamental step for others to love us in turn. Love your body, your faults, your qualities, all the things that you are passionate about, the way you smile, and walk the path of life.

"When I was 5, my mother always told me that happiness was the key to life. When I went to school, they asked me what I wanted to be when I grow up. I said "happy." They told me that I did not understand the instructions and I told them that they did not understand life."
—John Lennon—

Do you love as much as possible?
Loving yourself is fundamental for feeling good, for other people to love us, for enjoying life, and being happy.

It is a complex path, because we are often very critical of ourselves, sometimes becoming our worst enemy.

Self-esteem

Self-esteem is the evaluative perception of ourselves, that is, it is about how we see ourselves, how we value ourselves.
It is based on four fundamental pillars according to the Argentinian psychologist Walter Riso.

Here they are:
Self-conception: what we think of ourselves.
Self-image: the way we see ourselves.
Self-reinforcement: when we reward ourselves.
Self-efficacy: the confidence we have in ourselves.

To strengthen the four elements of self-esteem and to live in peace with ourselves, and to be happier, we suggest that you put in place some small strategies to teach you to love yourself and appreciate that there is good in you.

Don't compare yourself to others
Since adolescence, we are stuck in a process of depreciative analysis of our physique, which leaves us to think that there is always something missing so that we are perfect in our eyes.

We don't like our hair color, our legs, or our teeth. We strive to find ourselves a thousand and one faults. We also compare ourselves to others, who are always more beautiful than us, and that can do us a lot of harm.

The comparisons are negative. The concept of beauty varies from person to person, it is completely subjective. What we can consider beautiful, another person can see as ugly, and vice versa. This is why comparisons are simply useless.

"To want to be another person is to spoil the person you are. " -Marilyn Monroe

Discover and showcase everything you love at home. Do whatever you want with yourself, don't bend the way others would like you to be. If you feel good, that's all that matters.
There will always be someone more beautiful or uglier than you, but what matters is that your qualities make you unique.

Discover them and let them express themselves. Invent your own concept of beauty. The concept of beauty is not only subjective, but it also depends on personality. Many years ago, a woman, with white skin accomplished by "venetian ceruse" and rosy lips was considered beautiful, while the current canons of beauty are completely different.

So, the best thing to do is to build your own concept of beauty. In this sense, Walter Riso advises us to start in this way: "You can decide your own conception of beauty. It is not easy, but it is important to try to do it. To dress, do not obediently follow fashion by melting in a mold. To love yourself, you don't need to apply external concepts. You don't have to please someone in particular. No scientific theory justifies the predominance of one form of beauty over another. The important thing is not to be beautiful, but to love yourself."

Reward yourself

When our partner doesn't care about us, doesn't ask us how we're doing, doesn't call us, and doesn't care about us, it's hard to imagine love in the relationship we have with him. Hence why it is important to not give your full unconditional love to another person. I guarantee that person will most likely let you down.

Your unconditional love belongs to you! If you do not reward yourself, if you do not allow yourself a little time daily, if you do not express your feelings, your self-esteem will be nil or insufficient. Self-love, in principle, is no different from love for others. Take care of your body and mind, do things that you enjoy, and that please you. Smile and go outside to share your smile. If you like going to the movies, go there. If you love cycling, don't hesitate. If you like to read, go to your bookstore and treat yourself.

Eliminate repressive beliefs

According to Walter Riso, repressive beliefs prevent us from strengthening our self-esteem. There are four of them:

- The addiction cult: this is the cult that we devote to a whole series of behaviors that we consider to be habitual, that we feel obliged to have, but which do not allow us to innovate or change.

- The cult of rationalization: this cult leads us to be robots that evaluate feelings in a quasi-scientific way to see if they suit us. Certain things are not made to be thought, but to be felt.

- The cult of self-control: this is what makes us want to control all of our feelings and emotions. It is important to control yourself to avoid having destructive behaviors, but we must not fall into the repression of everything we feel.

- The cult of modesty: it can lead us not to value our successes and our efforts. It's not about bragging about our successes, but realistically acknowledging our potential, without apologies or feelings of guilt. This allows us to know how to value our qualities and to appreciate our efforts.

"If you cannot love yourself, you will find it difficult to love others because you will feel that the time and energy that you devote to another person, you do not even give to yourself. "-Bárbara De Angelisi-

Let yourself be loved

In today's society, everything is going far too quickly. We are all very independent and active, but we must stop for a moment and let ourselves be loved. If you feel bad, let others listen to you and take care of you.

If something is bothering you, share it and let others hug and kiss you. Feel the tenderness there is in each of their gestures and in each of their looks. Let yourself be loved.

The foundation of self-esteem

As I always explain, our identity and self-esteem are built from different sources. In my case, it is clear that the bashing I suffered for several years made its way into my head and convinced me, at least in part, that I had little value.

Who says lack of value also says lack of respect...?

In this context, when all facets of ourselves express the lack of esteem for what we are, it sends a clear message to others, even if this message is unconscious and is usually transmitted non-verbally. We convince others, without our knowledge, that we are not worth their respect! Self-esteem harmonizes our vision of ourselves, supports confidence, and helps us to assert ourselves. Several researchers in psychology have suggested that self-esteem moderates anxiety and is even a witness to our autonomy.

The signs of self-respect that promote respect for others
I would like to offer you some clues that will help you know if you really respect yourself. Read them well.

Do you recognize yourself? Otherwise, the rest of the article will provide you with tools and refer to resources to help you do that!

- Express our needs, our desires, our dreams.
- Express our emotions, our states, our mood.
- Express our ideas, our tastes, everything that defines us, and proves that we are proud of ourselves and that we are not afraid of the judgment of others.
- Accept our body and take good care of it (dressing well, for example).
- Be satisfied with what we are doing.
- Take our place in front of others without being aggressive or disrespectful (assertiveness).
- Being able to make choices and assume them.
- Do not feel guilty unnecessarily or judge yourself too harshly.
- Accept and find relevant marks of appreciation from others.
- To expect to be respected is to know that others will recognize our right to be who we are.
- Respect begins with ourselves, then comes respect from others

And this respect can, subsequently, open the way to dialogue, forgiveness, and play an important role in improving our daily lives. Here are examples of what self-esteem and self-respect lead to, and especially how to nurture and maintain them:

1. The ability to know us

It is about paying sufficient attention to ourselves to know who we are, through our values, our ways of reacting, our interests, etc., to feel good about what we are and to avoid confusion. Respecting ourselves then consists in doing what corresponds to what we are. It is consistency and authenticity, two ways of being that command great respect from others.

2. The ability to accept ourselves through our strengths and weaknesses

Are you perfect? No.

Neither am I.

It may seem trivial, but the simple fact of recognizing our imperfections and our perfectibility has several positive consequences: It promotes humility.

Humility feeds self-improvement: it is easier to improve when we know that we are not perfect than when we are full of pride and that we no longer believe that we have anything to learn...

- This takes the stress away from us: we are not perfect and need not be.
- This awareness helps us to recognize and appreciate who we are.
- This allows us to give less importance to what we may miss, precisely because we capitalize on what we have.

In short, as you can see, despite your faults, despite your gray areas, accepting what you are in your entirety rather than fighting against what you do not control will do you the greatest good.

This will help you respect yourself, which will positively influence the respect that others give you.

3. The possibility of comparing ourselves to others in a constructive and non-deprecative way

We cannot ignore others in our life. And as I said earlier, it was many of the other students in my high school that hurt others' self-esteem. But we were still young and impressionable. We had not yet reached our adult maturity.

This maturity comes with greater self-knowledge and better access to reason, to criticize the misconceptions represented by the gratuitous contempt that can come from others. Rest assured, if someone calls me all the names today, they won't do me the harm they could have done to me when I was 14... Others, therefore, play a big role in how we see ourselves. And to know us, we often compare ourselves. This comparison is positive if we are inspired by certain qualities that others have to give us avenues of improvement.

Unfortunately, we often make a monumental mistake, that of comparing ourselves overall to another person, by drawing a general conclusion like "He (she) is better than me."

This kind of conclusion is very effective in sabotaging the respect we have for ourselves because it leads us to want to be someone else. Not very good either for authenticity! Any comparison must, therefore, respect who we are despite the qualities we do not (yet) possess. This perspective eliminates unpleasant states like envy, dissatisfaction, and self-deprecation. Furthermore, comparing ourselves constructively with others helps us to cultivate respectful and conflict-free relationships. We accept ourselves and we accept others as they are.

In his book Self Deception and Self Under-standing, Mike Martin, author and professor at Chapman University (California), describes particularly well the adequacy that exists be-tween the values that govern our life, self-es-teem, and the possibility of asserting ourselves. and to make us respected. This quote from him is very logical and I have often meditated on it because I find that it sums up the dynamics of who we are particularly well:

"To live is to act; to act is to act for certain rea-sons; to see that our actions are based on good reasons consists of giving them a certain value, and identifying yourself with such acts is tacitly assuming value."

Self-affirmation

Assertiveness is the ability and the desire to as-sert who we are and to be respected. You should put yourself first and be respected for that. It involves affirming what is important to us without being afraid of seeing it rejected.

The ability to assert oneself thus requires the conviction that we have real value and the cer-tainty of being unique, free, capable of choos-ing and obtaining what we want.

To assert ourselves, we also sometimes have to do what we fear. For example, even if you are afraid to tell others what you think, you can still respectfully state your opinion. If you're worried that your ideas may be unattractive, you can start by expressing them without imagining that you will bore the gallery. When we respect ourselves, we subtly express to others the esteem we have for ourselves.

So, it's hard to assert yourself until you feel worthy of interest. Because respect for ourselves inspires respect for others. If we neglect ourselves, if we let others decide for us, if we don't put our will at the service of our identity, our freedom of action and our self-esteem will likely decrease.

You Deserve The Best

You deserve long love letters, letters that are addressed only to you... Because they describe you in every detail.

You deserve long messages, messages that no one else could send you... Because they mention all these little things that nobody notices, that even you don't notice... But that constitute the reasons why you are loved.

You deserve words that warm you up when it's cold and heal you when you're in pain. You deserve words that make you smile and remind you of how precious you are. You deserve sentences that testify to the love you have, that allow you to believe in yourself. You deserve calls that last for hours. Calls that let you know that no matter where you are, someone deeply needs you and cannot live without you. You deserve better than going to the local cafe. You deserve long conversations about the deeper meaning of life. You deserve that house and your dream car. You deserve that tropical vacation. You deserve great discussions about anything in your head and to be able to talk about everything, without censorship.

You deserve to be taken wherever you want to go to discover the things and places that matter to you. You deserve people who want everything with you, people who are the happiest in the world at the idea of parading by your side. people who are ready for big gestures, but who are also ready to spend an entire evening discussing with you what you want. You deserve people who take pride in introducing themselves to your friends and the world. You deserve to be the most beautiful thing that has happened to them. You deserve real relationships and real commitment.

You deserve genuine love, sincere love that goes beyond a few words on a screen, and a few emojis, a love that envelops your heart in sweetness and soothes your spirit. A love that does not give rise to doubts, questions, or fears in you. You deserve people who never make you wonder how long they will be there. People that keep you awake all night. Those who make you impatient to start your day, it is so magical and extraordinary.

You deserve the best in your life.

You deserve people who are ready to fight for you. People who don't use false pretenses and wobbly excuses to justify paying little attention to you. You deserve someone who always has time for you. You deserve to be someone's treasure, their most precious jewel (Whether or not you too are named after a gem), their reason for living, their reason for believing, and their reason for continuing. People who think of you in every decision they make. Finally, you deserve to tell yourself that love exists and that you have found it by loving yourself first.

Conclusion

It is generally fine for you to decline any meet-ups with your friends or any possible dates. It is more than alright for you to stop the whole world around you for a while. There are some days when you feel that you need to prioritize yourself and I honestly say go for it. Try to take as much time as you need in your bubble to get a rest from all of the chaos of this world.

Your soul is screaming for attention and it is normally important for you to attend to it. You must be the most important person in your life. **Remember that nobody is obliged to take care of your needs but you. You may think of others only when you've taken care of yourself.**

We sometimes busy ourselves with the problems of other people that we ignore our own. There is that sense of gratification when you try to manage to help someone out of their difficulties. As moral as it is to help others, please remember to never deprive your own needs. You should put yourself first.

Prioritizing yourself is a selfless act. You normally do not have to feel guilty about

it. When you are alone, you are allowed to do some reflection. It helps you re-assess your relationship with other people and your goals in life. Now, there are no voices around to dictate how you should live your life. You'll re-notice yourself and decide what is best for you. It allows you to improve your shortcomings and work on your strengths.

So, take this advice and move a step back and embrace the relationship you have with yourself. Learn to love yourself more. Learn to let go of all the things that are beyond your control. Therefore, the next time you want to ask someone how they are doing, stop for a second and ask *yourself* the same question.

Can I Ask For A Favor?

If you enjoyed this book, found it useful, or otherwise, I'd appreciate it if you would post a short review. I read all reviews personally so that I can continually write on topics closely pertaining to my interests and what people are wanting.

Thanks for your support!

Printed in Great Britain
by Amazon

86843913R10062